MW00653584

To

From

For
My Mother

Published by LONGSTREET PRESS, INC.
A subsidiary of Cox Newspapers,
A division of Cox Enterprises, Inc.
2140 Newmarket Parkway – Suite 118
Marietta, Georgia 30067

Copyright © 1996 by Lee J. Painter

All rights reserved. No part of this book may be reproduced in any form or by any means without the prior written permission of the Publisher, excepting brief quotations used in connection with reviews, written specifically for inclusion in a magazine or newspaper.

Printed in the United States of America
1st printing 1996
Library of Congress Catalog Card Number: 95-82233
ISBN 1-56352-295-0

Jacket design by Neil Hollingsworth
Book design and typesetting by Laura McDonald

Digital film prep and separations by Advertising Technologies, Inc., Atlanta, GA

Each Day is a Gift ...

. . . that's why it's called the present

Lee J. Painter

LONGSTREET PRESS
Atlanta, Georgia

Some days, even before my feet touch the floor, I allow responsibilities to hang around my neck like anchors and obligations to pull on me like tethers. Even before the day has really begun, I feel overworked and overwhelmed, unbalanced and off center.

And then, with a little luck and a little grace, I see the way the early morning light streams through the leaded window at the front door and makes a rainbow on the old oak flooring. Standing at my kitchen sink, I see rays of sunshine coming through the towering pines across the street. Those rays dance on the neighbors' roof, skip over the little creek, race up my yard, and pour through the mullioned windows. I hear a loved one's voice from the other room and a child's footsteps on the stairs.

The anchors begin to fall away. The tethers are snipped. And just as I felt weighted and torn before, I begin to feel light and centered. The footsteps remind me once again that we get only one chance to raise our children. The voice reminds me that love is a treasure. I see the neighbors and their children piling into their cars, and I am reminded that loyal and thoughtful friends are rare. And the light, spinning through prisms and making patterns on the floor, reminds me that each single day is a gift — that's why it's called the present.

I try to keep these reminders at hand as I move through the day, letting them warm my spirit just as the sunlight warmed my face in those early morning hours. I try to tuck them in my pockets and carry them with me just as I used

to pull an imaginary star from the air, place it my daughter's small hand, curve her fingers over the star, and tell her to hold it tight through the night. Sometimes I am successful. Other times I've forgotten all my blessings and treasures even before I'm out of the shower or have backed the car down the drive. Sometimes I don't even remember them again until the next morning.

Then, with a little luck and a little grace, I'm presented with them all once more. That's why each morning I vow to find one new "star" to hold in my hand, one new sliver of "light" to carry in my pocket to remind me still again that each day is a gift and I must not squander it.

That's why I vow each morning that today I will . . .

Remember that emotions are contagious.

Trust my instincts.

Listen to the trees as they bend with the wind.

Fish the streams that are close at hand.

Wind my grandfather's pocket watch.

Tread lightly on
what is fragile.

Watch a butterfly break
free of its cocoon.

Turn down the
volume of noise
in my life.

Be instructed
by the wisest, not
by the loudest.

Stop doing what
I'm supposed to do
and start doing what I
want to do.

Play ragtime piano.

Roast marshmallows on an open fire.

Remember that no one became good at anything overnight.

Call or visit the loved ones I've been too busy to see.

Stop saying that I'm too old or that it's too late.

Stop saying that I'm too young or that I'll get to the important things later.

Take a child camping on a clear cool night.

Reread the books I was too young to understand the first time.

Pick a handful of flowers for a sick friend instead of ordering a bouquet from a florist.

Remember that although suffering is universal, it's always brand-new to those who are grieving.

Pull up the covers
and take a nap on a cold,
winter afternoon.

Never stop trying to
make a contribution.

Empty my soul of insults too-long remembered.

Finally take that trip I've always wanted, no matter what the cost.

Imagine life in my neighbor's shoes.

Take a child to the country instead of the mall.

Slip out of the
house before everyone
else wakes up and take
a walk by myself
at dawn.

Memorize a poem.

Celebrate without envy the accomplishments of friends.

Play in the snow with the dogs and the children.

ROCKWELL KENT

Plant a garden
and share my harvest
with neighbors.

Walk barefoot down
the dirt roads of my
childhood.

Reconnect with
an old friend, no matter
how much time or
distance has come
between us.

Give sympathy more often than I ask for it.

Learn a new song . . . and sing it often.

Imagine what
it's like to be the
child instead
of the parent.

Sit down to a meal of fish that I have caught, corn and tomatoes that I have grown.

Have a special gathering of my family at some time other than the holidays.

Walk a fussy baby to sleep.

Open a child's mind to the magic of books.

WALTHER
FIRLE

Remember that calm and measured words are heard more clearly than shouted ones.

Let the children make a pie from scratch or bake a pan of brownies without worrying about the mess.

Give an exhausted parent an hour's relief.

Stay outside after dark with a child and look for constellations.

Acknowledge others' good points instead of searching for their faults.

Remember that any word or gesture can become a child's memory.

Light candles at dinner tonight for no special reason.

Eat a bag of peanuts at a minor league baseball game.

Learn the names of the flowers I pass each day on the side of the road.

Promise never to intentionally hurt another's feelings — and live up to it.

Ask an old person's advice.

Ask a teenager's advice.

Eat freshly-picked strawberries still warm from the sun.

Give someone a gift for no reason at all.

Invite an angel to climb my tree.

Watch a one-year-old take her first steps.

Never stop learning.

Have greens ready
to harvest at the
first frost.

Nurture even my
silliest aspirations.

Know intimately the lives of history's great men and women.

Tell a hilarious joke — at no one's expense.

Count the rings on an old stump.

Listen to Mozart on a Sunday morning.

Clean up all the messes
I've left behind me.

Go swimming
in the ocean on a
moonlit night.

Climb the hill
and touch the stones
of the Acropolis.

Celebrate the little
things.

Remember that sometimes it takes only one person to make a difference.

Judge tenderly,
or not at all.

Run like a child —
for the pure joy of it.

Pour a solid
foundation and build
with confidence.

Place my hands in potter's clay.

Sit under a covered porch on a summer morning and listen to the rain.

Stand in
a shower of leaves
on an October
afternoon.

Turn off the TV and put together a jigsaw puzzle with the kids, or play a game of Scrabble or Monopoly.

Say the right things for the right reasons.

Give my daughter all the time she deserves.

Remember those
who came before and
on whose shoulders
we stand.

Make a place that children love to visit.

Be quiet, and listen.

ILLUSTRATION CREDITS:

Page 5 — Carl Holsoe *A Woman Seated at a Table by a Window.* © Christie's, London/Superstock

Page 12 — John Hollis Kaufman *Zinnias.* © Private Collection/Superstock

Cover and page 21 — Rockwell Kent *Snow Fields (Winter in the Berkshires).* © National Museum of American Art, Washington, D.C./Art Resource

Page 29 — Walter Firle *A Good Book.* © Christie's, London/Superstock

Page 40 — Sir Edward Burne-Jones *Rudyard Kipling.* © National Portrait Gallery, London/Superstock

Page 49 — William Merritt Chase *At The Window.* © P. P. Ching/Superstock

Page 52 — Claude Monet *Poplars On The Epte.* © Private Collection/Superstock